10 Ways to Start Prepping Today

By Robert Paine

© **2014**

Are You and Your Family Ready to Survive the Next Disaster?

If you have ever thought about prepping, you have probably been a bit overwhelmed, at least once or twice. It can seem like a monumental task that will take too much work. Where do you start?

You have to start somewhere. You can start with these ten things. It isn't all about buying food and supplies. There is a lot of research and planning that goes into prepping. That is going to be where your prepping journey starts. Slow and easy is the way to go!

If you are interested in learning how to protect your family from any and all of the inevitable disasters that could potentially happen, this book is your first step to learning how to prepare for any emergency situation. Get started today!

Sign up for Robert's Mailing List to be notified of **New Releases** and **Special Sales**: http://eepurl.com/zvm11

10 Ways to Start Prepping Today

If you have ever thought about prepping, you have probably been a bit overwhelmed, at least once or twice. It can seem like a monumental task that will take too much work. Where do you start? You see these pictures of food storage shelters or pantries that have enough food to last a family a year or more and it can be daunting. Maybe you have read stories of people creating these bunkers or hideouts in the woods with a huge cache of emergency supplies. You are probably thinking, "That will take me forever! I don't even know where to begin." Well, like a wise man once said a few hundred years ago, "Rome wasn't built in a day," and neither are those vast emergency food storages.

You have to start somewhere. Somewhere small. Somewhere easy. You can start with these ten things, today. It isn't all about buying food and supplies. There is a lot of research and planning that goes into prepping. That is going to be where your prepping journey starts. Grab a pen and paper and prepare to write down the thoughts that pop into your head as you read along. Remember, your prepping is best done in manageable, bite-size pieces. It will be less overwhelming and you won't feel like you are trying to climb a mountain. Slow and easy is the way to go!

1) Research and Educate Yourself About Prepping.

Fairly obvious for a first step, no? Still, you'd be surprised how many so-called Preppers have never even read anything on the subject! Yes, it sounds tedious, but you are going to discover there is a plethora of information available about prepping, everywhere you look. Books, movies, TV shows, podcasts, and on and on. Some of it is helpful while some of it is really quite pointless and a waste of time. You need information that will prove of some value to you. Prepping is an activity that requires careful consideration. Every family and every individual will have different needs. When you are looking for materials about prepping, follow those that offer real solutions and suggestions that you can apply to your family. If something doesn't apply to you and your situation, skip it. If you live in the city, look for prepping materials geared toward the urban prepper. Reading about raising cattle and farming isn't going to be of much use to you if you plan on living in your high-rise apartment in the middle of the city.

Ebooks (like mine! And many others!) are great for finding information quickly. However, you will want to have print copies of the research you uncover as much as possible. What are you gonna do if the grid goes down?! Part of prepping is preparing to deal with long term power outages, which means your Kindle or Nook isn't going to work so well. All that beautiful information will be out of reach. Now is the time to really get organized. It is a good idea to keep all your research in a binder. Take the time to keep it all straight, with tabs and everything else you can think of. This will make it easy for you to quickly flip to the information you need when you are in a rush. A binder is a great way to keep all your research together in one place. Your family will also be able to find what they need in case you are not immediately available. Keep your binder with your emergency preps for easy access.

Don't stop at just one resource. You will discover there are a lot of really good ideas out there. Nobody preps the same. Some ideas will work for you and your family, while some will not. Learn from other people's mistakes. There is no need to reinvent the wheel. Again, I know it may seem really obvious, but don't skip this vital first part of prepping: Do your research and educate yourself!

2) Create, Study, and Practice your Overall Emergency Plan (and then do it all again!)

You know those little maps on the back of hotel room doors that indicate where you are in the building? The maps have a red line that indicates the path for you to escape in case of an emergency. Those maps are there for a reason. When there is a situation that threatens your life and that of your family, you tend to get a little crazy. You could end up running in circles because you are panicking. Prepping eliminates those little panic attacks that threaten your life and sends you running in circles.

You need an emergency plan for your family. A map, of sorts, that tells you all what steps you're going to take in case of an emergency. This is going to require you to think of all the little details that are likely to arise in a true emergency. All of the things that you will be too busy to think about when the situation actually arises. Now is the time to think about them and to plan for them. Brainstorm different plans and write them down. Put them away for an hour and come back to them and review your different strategies. Do you see any flaws or pieces of the puzzle missing? For example, if you are going to be hunkering down in your basement, who is going to ensure the front door is locked and barricaded? Who is going to make sure each of the children in the family gets to the basement safely? What are you going to do with your pets? Who will be in charge of doing a head count? Does the entire family know they are supposed to get to the basement when you give the word?

Pick each member of your family's brains for their best ideas.

You cannot do it all and you don't want to do it alone. Get everyone in your household involved. The more people you have, the more chances you have to catch important things that you may have missed if you are trying to do it all alone. You need to rely on every source available. Once you have come up with what you think is a pretty good emergency plan, do a run through. Practice and drill it as though the event is actually taking place. Everyone needs to approach this with a serious mindset. This is going to be a bit rough the first few times through – that's okay. Expect the family to be running in circles the first couple of times you test out your plan. Each time should get a little easier and a little more orderly. This is what you are trying to achieve. Practice makes perfect! That perfect plan you put together is going to have holes in it when you actually put it into action. This is why you are drilling it.

You absolutely must physically practice your emergency plan. This is the only way to discover those little hiccups in the plan. Time yourself and the family. How long does it take to get everybody into the basement? Are there things you can do to make the retreat go a little smoother and faster? Once you have established a plan, you will want to practice at least once a month to keep everybody familiar with it. If you move a piece of furniture or add a new member to the family, you need to tweak your plan. Try practicing for different scenarios. If the grid goes down and there is no power, how will your reactions be different? If there is a flood and water is in the basement, making it unusable, where will you go as a backup? The more scenarios you practice and prepare for, the better off everyone in the family will be. You will feel confident that everyone will know what to do, regardless of the reason that the plan needs to be put into place. And really, isn't that what prepping is all about?

3) Create a Bug Out Bag (BOB)

Your next step is to start putting together a bug out bag, or at least deciding what you need to start gathering to put in your bug out bag. A bug out bag is essentially a backpack or duffel filled with tools you would need to survive out in the open. Typically, the bag should be filled with items that will keep you alive as you travel from point A to point B or if you are stranded somewhere. A 3-day supply of food (and water, if possible) is typical for a bug out bag. The bags are not meant to sustain an entire family for a full month, but each bag should support one person for up to 72 hours.

Bug out bags must be fairly lightweight so they don't hinder you. You need to be able to move freely, quickly, and easily while carrying your BOB. A bag that is loaded with everything but the kitchen sink is like an albatross around your neck and could actually put your life in jeopardy. You cannot maneuver quickly when you are carrying around 100 pounds of gear. It could slow you down, cause you to trip and fall or strain your back. All of which are extremely serious and potentially life-threatening in a survival situation.

Do some research on the various types of bags that can be used as a bug out bag. A framed backpack is ideal for packing the most gear. Look for them at camping stores or hiking outlets. General sporting goods stores may also carry them. However, the downside is that these packs tend to be rather expensive. If you can swing it or find one that is on sale or possibly used, definitely go for it. Their design makes them hands down the best choice for a BOB.

The internal frame helps distribute the weight of the pack across your hips and shoulders. They tend to be way more comfortable to pack around. If you think your situation will call for you to hike several miles, or if you live anywhere that isn't flat, with some hills or even mountains, you should consider investing in one of these packs.

If you can't find, can't afford, or simply don't want a hiking pack, then a standard backpack will suffice. However, you will want to find one that has the hip belt and pads. It may not seem like much when you try it on at the store, but when you are walking several miles with a pack weighing more than 30 pounds, you will appreciate the extra padding and support on your hips and lower back. You will also want to look for a bag that has plenty of internal and external pockets. This will help keep your gear organized. Places to clip gear to the outside of the pack is also essential. You want to have easy access to things like a whistle and flashlight or knife. Clipping them outside your pack makes them quick and easy to grab when the situation demands it. You don't want to have to stop, open the pack, and fumble around for something that you may need in a split second.

Usually it's safe to say: Don't waste your time with duffel bags, suitcases or other bags that require you to use your hands to carry them. They are much more trouble than they are worth. You will offset your center of gravity and struggle to walk. You will need to stop anytime you want to get something out of the bag. They're often awkward or cumbersome to move quickly with, or to scale any sort of terrain. You will need your hands free to carry a flashlight or other tools, and these types of bags simply don't allow for those situations easily enough.

So, you got your bag picked out – now what? Now you need to figure out what you're going to load it up with! At a minimum, your bug out bag should include the following;

- Matches, flint steel, or lighter
- Flashlight
- Whistle
- Energy bars
- Basic first aid kit
- Emergency blanket
- Cordage i.e. paracord
- Canteen
- Water purification tablets and perhaps one or two bottles of water
- Knife
- Another weapon is optional. A can of Mace, pepper spray or a taser are all great, cheap options if you are not comfortable carrying a gun.

Those are some of the very basic items you will need. Of course, it's not a complete list of everything you may need or want – that will be very situation-dependent. You will want to tweak your bug out bag to suit your needs and the climate you live in. Rain gear, extra socks, a hat and gloves are all options. Have some options for winter as well, if you live somewhere that this will be an issue. You don't want to pack the perfect bug out bag, only to find out that you have to use it in the middle of December and, whoops, you didn't pack any winter gear!

If you require prescription medications include a supply of your medicines in the bag. If you have a serious allergy, buy an extra Epi-Pen to keep in your bug out bag. Each member of the family should have a bug out bag. Children's bug out bags will obviously be much smaller, but they should have some of the basic gear just in case they get separated from you. Make sure you choose a backpack that is the right size for your child. Adult packs are not suitable for a child's small size. Having a child help brainstorm what they should pack, picking out the perfect bag for them, and having them help pack it up nice and tight, is a great way to get children involved and help them feel like they are really an important part of the process (because, they are!). Giving them some control over their bug out bag will really help cement this in their minds.

4) Choose Your Locations (Main, Backup, and Backup for the Backup!)

Part of prepping is always having a backup plan. And then having a backup to your backup. You cannot predict what will happen or how it will affect you. You can, however, prepare for almost anything. That old saying, "Prepare for the worst and hope for the best," applies to prepping. You hope you won't have to leave the comfort of your house with all of your things, but there is a real possibility you will have to leave it all behind. You need a rally point, so to speak, for your family to retreat to if your home is compromised. A meet up place. Somewhere that everyone will remember in any time of crisis.

Many preppers living in the city choose to have a location somewhere outside of town to retreat to. That's fine, if you're able to get out of town, once something goes bad. Have a backup plan for another location in the city, if all exits are blocked. Ideally, you want somewhere that is close enough for you to walk to if necessary, but far enough out of the city (or hidden enough inside of the city) that you won't have to worry about dealing with too many unscrupulous people trying to get to your emergency food supply or any other of your items. This is where you will store the majority of your emergency supplies. The bug out bag we talked about in the last section is what will sustain you on your journey to reach the second location.

If you already live outside of town, you will probably still need to have a second location picked out. Maybe you live in tornado alley or near a nuclear reactor. You need to have a second location just in case your home is destroyed or it isn't safe to be in. This is also helpful for your family members just in case you are separated or are not together when it is time to bug out. Make sure you designate a route for each family member to follow as well as a backup route in case the first is compromised. If a bridge is out or the traffic is too bad, you need to have a second option. Think back to the map on the back of the hotel door. You need a clear route. The shortest route is always better, but it may not always be an option.

Choose a second location that is relatively out of sight. If you can invest in fencing and other security measures, it would be a good idea. Set up a solar panel or two as an alternative energy means. Start collection rainwater. Do what you can today to make that location as safe and as comfortable as possible. Visit the location from time to time with your family to make sure they are familiar with it. Practice getting there during different seasons, different times of the day, and in different scenarios. When disaster strikes, it can be extremely difficult to deal with emotionally. Having a familiar place to hole up in will provide comfort at a time when it is sorely needed. If you have children, make sure you have a few of the toys they like and any special blankets or other comfort measures available. If you have pets, don't forget to stock some kibble or any other supplies, if you plan on taking them with you.

The second location is one that you will want to keep fairly under wraps. You don't want to advertise the fact to neighbors, co-workers and others who are not a part of your prepping plan. People will get desperate in the aftermath of a disaster if they have not done their own prepping. They will be willing to do things they wouldn't normally do to stay alive. Keep the second location known only to those who you trust the most, and only those who you wouldn't mind trying to survive with, if it comes to that!

5) Create or Update Your Emergency Contact List (and make sure everyone in your family knows it!)

You will want to create an emergency contact list. Most of us rely on our cell phones to store all of our contacts. Many of us don't even know our parent's or kids' phone numbers by memory. We simply find their name in our phone books and push a button. If your cell phone is broke or the battery is dead, you won't have any way to access those numbers. What if the grid is down – how will you contact anyone?

Take the time today to create a list of important names, numbers, and addresses. Print copies to keep in your emergency binder and give one to each member of the family. It is a good idea to write the numbers and addresses on a notecard and seal the card with clear contact paper to protect it from moisture. For little kids, write the information on a piece of fabric and either sew it into their backpack or inside their jacket. If disaster strikes when you are away from your child, you want them to be able to contact you or call for help.

There are some key people that you will want to have contact information for, above all others. Of course, the people you contact and the order in which you call them will depend on what type of disaster you are dealing with. Some examples include:

- Sheriff/state police numbers besides 911
- Family member who lives in another area to check in with
- Each family member's individual number

- School numbers for each child
- Daycare phone number
- Work phone numbers
- Local hospital number
- Red Cross

You have to assume emergency services are going to be taxed following a disaster. Calling 911 may not work. You need to be able to call the police directly. If something happens and you need to pick up your kids at a different time or you need to have somebody else pick up the child, you will want to have the school number. The Red Cross will likely be called in within a few days. They will have a number for family members to call and register with so you can all get in touch just in case you lose contact with your loved ones. Addresses are equally important to have. In the even the phone grid goes down, you need to have a way to reach your family or other important contacts. Having phone numbers will not be enough in these situations, so make sure you have addresses as well, at least for a few vital people or places. As we said before, have a backup for your backup – you never know which one you'll need!

6) Figure Out Who Will Be a Part of Your Overall Survival Plan (family, friends, neighbors)

Many preppers are very secretive about their prepping. They hide it, lie about it and do their best to make excuses as to why there are 15 gallons of water stashed under the sink. Sometimes that can be a good strategy. Then again, sometimes that can backfire. It is best if you include at least a few people that you can trust in your planning. You can't do it all alone, no matter how much you believe in yourself. You don't want to me a lone survivor. It would be extremely difficult to take care of everything needed for survival on your own. There are simply too many factors to consider. Too many variables. Too many small, tiny things that could go wrong if you're all by yourself. There is also the fact it would be pretty lonely. Who knows how long a disaster scenario will last – do you really want to be all by yourself for what could turn out to be a very, very long time indeed?

Your immediate family, spouse, kids and anybody else who lives in the home should all be included in the planning process, at the very minimum. You need to talk with them about what you are doing, why you are doing it, and how they should all be able to get involved. Talk them through each step of the plan so they can be involved and prepared to jump right in without you having to take the time to explain the what and why. There is always a possibility you will not be home to act as the coordinator when disaster strikes. They need to know what to do to get your plans in motion, and where and how they will meet up with you later. You also have to consider the possibility of you being injured and unable to activate the plan of action. If you're not around, surely you still want your family to survive, right?!

If you have friends or neighbors that you trust, you can include them in your plan. Sometimes your skills can benefit each other in ways that you wouldn't have even thought of. Imagine if you are an expert gardener and your neighbor is quite the handyman. You are setting yourself up for success when you put together a team of individuals with different areas of expertise. You will be able to complement each other, which will aid in your survival. Divide and conquer is a very effective way to tackle all the little jobs that will need to be handled after a disaster.

It is also helpful to include others in the early stages of your planning process so you can bounce ideas off of each other. Sometimes your initial plan may have holes in it that you wouldn't be able to identify without a different perspective. Having another set of eyes to look over your plans, share their plans, and expose you to new ideas, can really be beneficial for your overall prepping strategy. Choose who you will involve in your prepping process wisely. Make sure they are people you can trust, as much as possible. Even still, don't give all of your plans away to anyone except your family and closest confidants. It would be wise to keep some pertinent details, like your second location or hidden stash of money, to yourself. Unfortunately, you can't always trust everybody; your family would be the exception.

Assign tasks for each person involved in your prepping. If

you are involving neighbors or friends and family, consider planning monthly or weekly meetings to talk about what you have done and what needs to be done. This is a great way to pool resources and take some of the financial burden off of yourself. It also keeps you focused on short-term goals that will help you achieve your long-term survival needs. You will have the benefit of using ideas from your fellow preppers. People can get pretty resourceful and there are often little tips or tricks that you wouldn't have thought of yourself. You want every advantage possible and if that means borrowing ideas from your fellow prepper, so be it. We all have the same goal and we all can learn a lot from each other.

7) Start Stockpiling Basic Food and Water (Start Early, Stock Often)

This is the part you have been waiting for! Or, at least, the part you knew was fairly obvious. You can't be a prepper unless you actually prep food and water, right? Right you are! You need to start thinking about what it is you want to store in case of an emergency, and what you really, definitely, absolutely *need* to store. Don't buy a bunch of canned spinach and beets that your family doesn't like just because they are super cheap. One of the most important rules of preparing a food storage is to only store what you would eat today. Your taste buds are not going to change just because there is an emergency. You are not suddenly going to decide anchovies are your favorite food. Don't waste your money on food that will leave your family longing for the good ol' days, *when* there are equally good choices. Sure, if you're all starving and haven't eaten in days following a disaster, you'll eat beets or anchovies in a heartbeat! But, if you could have spent $0.10 extra and gotten canned tuna instead, which you all love, doesn't it make sense to go for that option now?! Yes, of course it does.

You will need to come up with a plan of action to build up your food storage. What is your goal? How far in advance do you have the capabilities to prep for? How much space is in your prepping pantry? A good way to start is by planning a 3-month food storage, as a minimum. This helps you build up to the 1-year supply that many preppers aim for. You will want to do some basic math when it comes to planning how much food you need, depending on how many members of your family and your ages. You can go about this in couple of different ways.

The first would be to focus solely on calories. Technically, in survival mode, you are not eating for joy; you are eating to stay alive and healthy. You only need a certain amount of calories per day to do this. Plan on each family member eating 2000 calories per day (though they could easily get by on less, depending on age, size, gender, etc). Take a look at some of the food labels on the items your family likes or regularly eats. How much would a person need to eat to reach their daily calorie requirement? Are there better choices (cheaper, healthier) that could reach those goals more easily? Are there other options that have a longer shelf life and would be a much better fit for a prepping pantry? These are the types of questions to ask as you narrow down the types of foods you want to start buying and storing.

The second option would be to examine how much food you typically serve your family at each meal. Do you use one, two or three cans of soup to satisfy the family at lunch? Multiply that number by let's say 12, assuming you would serve that meal once a week for 12 weeks. How much rice do you usually go through in, say, a month? Focus on the most shelf-stable items and the ones that are most easily storable. You want to build the foundation of your pantry based off of these types of items. Many people make the mistake of not looking far enough ahead. For example, you say your family loves sandwiches and eats them every single day for lunch? So you want to store a couple loaves of bread? Forget it! Do you know how quickly bread goes bad? It's not even worth storing one loaf (unless you plan on eating it before the week is out!) So don't always focus on the things your family loves and eats the most; focus on the things with the longest shelf life!

Along the same lines - don't make the dangerous mistake of storing 100 cans of refried beans or chicken noodle soup and assume your family can live on the same meal every single day for a few months. There is a very real thing called food fatigue that can develop from eating the same food, day in and day out. Food fatigue causes intestinal upset and could ultimately lead to dehydration. That is not something you want to be dealing with when water is going to be in short supply. Buy with some variety and plan on serving different foods as frequently as it is viable to do so. Your taste buds, and your tummy, will thank you.

That brings us to our next topic—water storage. Everyone knows that we need water to survive, but how much is actually enough? It's safe to say you need, at the bare minimum, one gallon of water per day for each member of the family. If you plan on keeping your pets with you, you need to factor in their water needs as well. If you can't store enough water for your family, you need to store a water purification method to clean the water you gather. ALL water you collect is considered dangerous to drink without purifying first. So, how to go about collection and storing all of that water?

You have plenty of options to storing water. As part of your planning process, investigate some of the various ways you can gather or simply store water, like rain barrels and stackable water walls, which are 3-gallon square jugs that fit together to form a solid wall. This can be a huge space saver and gives you the luxury of being able to take an empty container off the wall so you can refill it whenever it is needed.

Take a walk around your neighborhood or the location you will be hunkering down in to find the nearest water sources. Ideally, you should look for water that is within a few miles of your abode. You don't want to be hauling water several miles each way on a daily basis. It could be dangerous and it will tax your energy. Look for streams or river, or sources of fresh water. If the only options are lakes or salt water, you are definitely going to need to have a large stock of water purification tablets in your storage pantry. These can be found in camping or outdoor sports stores, as well as in many places online. They typically have a fairly long shelf life, so feel safe loading up on as many as you think you will need. And then, when you have that number calculated, add on a few more, for extra measure! You can never be too safe when it comes to planning your water supplies – if you fail on that prep, nothing else will matter.

8) Prep Your Body and Mind!

Speaking of walking to collect water and then carrying back a 5-gallon jug of water - could you even do it? In your current state, would you get tired? Are you in decent physical condition? One of the major parts of prepping that many tend to overlook is the sheer physical nature of surviving. Lets face it: right now, we have it pretty easy. We turn on the tap when want water, we turn on the heater when we are cold, and when we are hungry, we open the freezer and pop something into the microwave. In a post-traumatic event world, ALL of those luxuries will be gone. If you want water, you have to find it and clean it. If you are cold, you have to find and chop the wood to build a fire. If you are hungry, you have to actually prepare a meal and either eat it cold or build a fire to cook it. It will take a lot longer than what you are accustomed to, and it will require a whole heck of a lot more energy than we ever use on those same tasks right now. It only makes sense, then, that now is the perfect time to get your body and mind in order, so that you'll be able to do all those necessary tasks to survive.

You need to get yourself and your whole family in good physical condition so you all are better able to handle the physical demands of life without electricity, running water or transportation. If you are overweight and are not currently active, you need to change it, now. Can you physically walk 10 miles or swing an axe in your current physical shape? If you can't, you need to start walking a little every day. Start building up your stamina so you are ready. Start small, but start today. Get the whole family involved. If you have little ones, you may have to carry them if you have to bug out to another location. Consider getting a wagon or cart that you can pull the little ones in.

If you have knee problems or other issues that will give you trouble in a physical world, keep a knee brace, back brace or whatever on hand to help aid you. Some of us are not quite as youthful as we once were, but there are ways to accommodate those little hiccups.

Part of your conditioning should include tasks that you would likely need to do in a survival situation. Things like chopping wood, carrying water, gardening, building a fire and walking long distances over hills are all likely activities when you are living in a world turned upside down. If I had to guess, I bet you currently don't do many, if any, of these vital activities. You can't just expect to magically jump into action, physically and mentally, when you haven't practiced any of those important tasks, can you? Of course not! You plan your prepping so thoroughly that you owe it to yourself to make sure you're in physical shape to be able to carry out your plans. Prepare yourself today so you are not struggling at a time when you simply cannot afford to be down and out.

9) Begin Getting Your Money and Finances in Shape (Prep Your Budget!)

There are plenty of scenarios that could thrust the world into something from the Dark Ages. Not every scenario will necessarily result in a collapse of the financial system. That means those bills you have today are still going to be there when things *do* get crazy. The last thing you want to deal with is a bill collector hunting you down and demanding payment. Can you survive both physically and financially?

You need to do your best to get your finances in shape now. Eliminate as much debt as you can. Make a concerted effort to manage your finances better. Live within your means. Don't go into debt in order to prep. If you currently live paycheck to paycheck, take a hard look at your existing expenses and find ways to cut costs.

Prepping, like buying food, water and other supplies, will take money to do. You don't want to max out your credit cards trying to stock up on things. The best way to create a healthy food storage that will sustain your family is to do it a little at a time in a way you can afford. Buy a few extra cans of food each time you go grocery shopping and add them to your food storage. Cut coupons. Buy things on sale. Adopt thrifty shopping habits and you will be so much better off.

Putting the family on a budget that frees up some of your current monthly income to put towards prepping is crucial. Often times, we say "Oh, we can buy that next week or next month when we don't have this bill or that bill." Guess what? There are always going to be those little bills that pop up. You'll never start prepping if you use this mindset. You have to change your lifestyle a bit to get out of debt and stay out while contributing to your emergency storage plan.

If you have extra "stuff" lying around the house just taking up space, consider having a yard sale to get rid of the stuff while making some extra cash. Use the cash to pay off a debt or to put towards buying food for your emergency storage. Tighten up your expenditures by cooking meals at home and making every dollar stretch. If you don't have to buy new—don't. Buy used and save some money. Work to get every last bit of use out of your tools, clothing, shoes and so on. Make leftovers a weekly meal instead of throwing them out.

Many preppers are investing in gold and silver coins to use as currency in a world that has suffered an economic collapse. This is a good idea. To afford those gold and silver coins, you are going to have to find room in your budget to do so. Don't be afraid to offer to trade things you have for gold and silver. Bartering is going to be the way of the future so it doesn't hurt to start learning the ropes today.

10) The Family that Preps Together, Survives Together!

You may discover certain family members are not on board with your desire to being prepping. They make be skeptical or they may just not understand your mindset in the least. You may be ridiculed and called names and teased about the sky falling and so on. So be it. You are trying to do something that will save your family's life. It may take some effort to convince some members of the family, but you have to try. People outside your immediate family will likely have an opinion about your "crazy ideas," but let it roll off your shoulders. When things do go sideways, they will be knocking on your door begging for help. You'll be the one prepared.

If somebody is adamant they don't want to be involved in learning various ways to start a fire or how to purify water, that's fine. Try getting them involved in preparing a food storage that will keep the family fed for a few months. Ask them what they're interested in and tailor their involvement towards those ends. You don't have to tell them you are prepping for nuclear fallout or some other disaster that may scare them. Tell them you are preparing for the possibility you may be without work or somebody may get very ill and the hospital bills will make it difficult to put food on the table.

Some members may be hesitant to buy into prepping simply because they don't want to think about such frightening scenarios that could leave the world as they know it in upheaval. Try to remove the fear by focusing on the food or prep items themselves and not the whys. Ask each member of the family what their favorite food is or what kind of food would they want to cat if they couldn't leave the house for a week. Make it into a game or a fun thought exercise. They'll be much more likely to participate if you don't make it all about the doom and gloom situations.

Bring up some real-life scenarios that have happened, like Hurricane Katrina, Hurricane Sandy or the earthquake in Haiti. Point out that those people were forced to go without for several days. Plenty of people died while waiting for emergency services. They suffered through an already horrible situation. If the people had planned ahead and had enough food and water, their suffering wouldn't have been nearly as bad. Natural disaster can strike anywhere at any time. Try to get your family to realize that you want them to be safe and comfortable in case something does happen. It isn't crazy!

Start out small and slowly work them into prepping. Picking food they want on the shelves and helping you organize is one way to work them into prepping. Make it an adventure when you talk about the different routes you would take in case you had to leave your home to a second location. Make your practice runs more about spending time together as a family rather than preparing for disaster. They will be learning the route without getting hung up on why they are learning it.

Lastly, don't push. If you have somebody that is truly reluctant, don't force the issue. Make sure they know where to go and what to do in case of emergency, but don't expect them to do much in the way of helping you prepare. Everybody comes to the understanding that prepping is a lifesaving tool in their own time.

Don't let it discourage you.

Conclusion

So there you have it. 10 concrete things that you can get started on today to make sure you and your loved ones are heading down the right path. They aren't huge, grand ideas. They are small, simple steps that you can easily start on today. They don't require a ton of money, or a ton of time. They just require you to be focused, dedicated, and to really want to take the first steps towards securing your future.

Prepping often gets a bad rap these days. People have a lot of pre-conceived ideas of it. Most of them are wrong. Prepping isn't crazy. Prepping isn't the most difficult thing a family can do. It doesn't have to be complicated. It doesn't have to be expensive. It can even be fun! The most important thing is that you simply start. Start now. There's no better time! As they say, the earlier you start, the better off you'll be when you really need it.

Good luck, fellow Preppers!

*****

If you've enjoyed this book, **please** consider leaving a review and letting others know what you thought!

Sign up for Robert's Mailing List to be notified of **New Releases** and **Special Sales**: http://eepurl.com/zvm11

No Spam – he promises!

Other Books by Robert Paine:
Prepper's Pantry: A Survival Food Guide
The Survivalist Cookbook - Recipes for Preppers
Prepping 101: A Beginner's Survival Guide
The Dead Road: The Complete Collection

www.ingramcontent.com/pod-product-compliance
Lightning Source LLC
Chambersburg PA
CBHW070524290526
45790CB00003B/1293